The Father's Day Stones

...A Small Treasure Hunt Story

By Pete Van Passion

Independently published

ISBN: 9798745354533

Copyright © 2004 Brian G. LaPlante, Jr.

All rights reserved, solely by Brian G. LaPlante, Jr. No part of this publication may be copied or reproduced in whole or in part, stored in retrieval system, or transmitted in any form or by any means, electronic, mechanical, photocopying, recorded, or otherwise without the prior written consent of Brian G. LaPlante, Jr.

All images contained herein are either the property of Brian G. LaPlante, Jr., and/or in some cases, sourced with permission from online, royalty free stock imagery.

Acknowledgements:

This book is dedicated to fathers, sons, daughters, and mothers all around the world who take time to honor and celebrate fatherhood …no matter what story or scenario befits us. Being a father is easy…being a good father is a different story for everyone. Special thanks to 407 and Lucie RN, for without them I would not be here. It has been said it takes a village to raise a child. Blessed are you who have a father, or father figure in your life to honor. If you don't, or you no longer have a father figure in your life, don't despair…you will always have the greatest father of all to celebrate… God.

Other books by Pete Van Passion:

A Little Something for Soulmates…V.1…Short wisps of words and art to share with the love of your life. ISBN#: 9798717366281

Way, way down deep from within the great hidden Underground Kingdom, during a time of love and kindness, a king and queen gave birth to a child - to cherish, to guide, to hold and to love.

The king and queen took the newborn child to the tallest stalagmite in the Underground Kingdom, and raised the child up high over their heads and named the baby "Geo", and proclaimed, "You are our future! The great namesake from which mountains shall rise and pastures shall flourish wherever you may tread."

The king and queen made it a point to show Geo everything in the Kingdom.

Luke 1:14

Every Father's Day, the king took little Geo to the edge of the magnificent Kingdom to play where there was a great glass Dome Barrier to the outside world. Directly below the giant Dome Barrier, lay some plain and simple looking stones. One day, Geo reached down and picked up one of the stones that stood out.

"What is this, Father? I have never seen it before," said Geo.

"This is a stone, and it is from one of the Six Seas of Success. This particular stone is found in the Sea of Courage. Without it, a person can never truly stand up for themselves or others," responded the king.

"Thank you, Father. Can you hold this stone for me until I am ready?" asked Geo.

The youngster then placed the stone in the king's hand and closed it.

They walked around a bit longer and then turned back toward the Kingdom to behold all of its splendor. Before they left, they agreed to come back every Father's Day. Then, they set off back towards the Kingdom.

Joshua 1:9, Deut 31:6

The following year, as planned, Geo and the king hiked back to the same place – the edge of the magnificent Underground Kingdom. And again, Geo found another interesting stone and picked it up.

"What is this stone?" Geo asked.

"Ah, yes, Geo, this stone is from the Sea of Compassion. Without this, no person will ever truly know their own heart, or the heart of another," said the king.

"Can you hold it for me until I am ready?" asked Geo.

The child again placed the stone in the king's hand before starting their way back toward the Underground Kingdom.

Before they entered the Kingdom, Geo saw another stone that looked similar to the Stone of Courage. The child bent down with curiosity to pick it up.

"Is this one also from the Sea of Courage, Father?" Geo asked.

"No," said the king, but it is just as important. It is from the Sea of Confidence. Without it, any courage that you have might be overcome by fear," answered the king.

Geo nodded and then placed the stone in the king's hands as they continued back down the countryside.

Psalm 37:26, Psa 103:13, Psa 145:8, Matt 5:7, Jeremiah 29:11, 2 Cor 7:4

A few more years had passed, and they once again made their annual pilgrimage to the spot next to the great glass Dome Barrier to the outside world. This time, Geo reached down and picked up two stones.

"I don't recognize these stones. From where did they come, Father?" Geo asked.

"Let me look...indeed...yes, these are also found in one of the Six Seas of Success. This one is found in the Sea of Commitment. Without it, no person's dream can ever make it through the Forest of Disappointment. The other one is from the Sea of Capability. Without it, a dream might take a lot longer to find its way out of that forest," said the king.

Geo smiled and placed the two stones in the king's hands and closed his palms just like before.

"Can you hold them until I'm ready, Father?" the growing child asked.

"Of course I can, Geo," said the king. "You are certainly finding some very valuable stones that might come in handy someday."

The king placed them in his pouch as they moved on.

Luke 8:15, Rom 5:3-4, Ruth 3:11

Of a sudden, the ground gave a big rumble and the entire Kingdom began to shake. Before the king could chase down curious Geo, the giant Dome Barrier breached and up went Geo, straight towards the cracked opening to the outside world.

"Don't worry, Geo. Either I will come and find you, or you can always come back through once the wind has died down and the quake has stopped. Just try to relax, be strong and enjoy the journey for now. You will be fine," reassured the king.

"But what if too much time passes, Father, and we both grow older? How will I recognize you?" Geo asked.

"That's easy…you will always recognize me by knowing my most valuable possessions! Let me show you!" shouted the king.

Before the king could pull the stones from his pocket to show Geo, the young child spiraled up and out through the broken glass Dome, exiting the Barrier with a big smile, and then disappeared.

The king sighed and scratched his head, wondering how he was going to get up through the Dome Barrier now to find Geo. The hole was way too high and far too small through which to pass.

"Perhaps Geo will return after becoming bored with the outside world, or maybe even miss us. I'll just wait here for a while," the king nervously thought to himself. "What ever shall I tell the queen?"

Luke 15:4

As promised, the king waited a little while, and a little while longer…

…And a little while longer……and a little while longer, and longer…returning every day until almost thirty years had passed!

In doing so, the king and queen lost all of their wealth and possessions trying to drill a larger hole through the Barrier so they could go up and out into the outside world to look for Geo. But sadly, they had failed.

All this time, Geo had been so busy exploring and experiencing the new world, and forgot all about the king and queen.

Through hard work and doing the right thing, the industrious young Geo had grown up to be a very generous, powerful, respected, and honorable member of the outside world, having given away much wealth to help others. Geo had even married and the new couple now had a child of their own. It was then that Geo thought of the beloved king and queen who were most certainly wondering about their long lost child.

"I must find my parents. I am going back down deep into the hidden Underground Kingdom to find them," declared Geo.

Matt 7:7, Jer 29:13, Psa 53:2, Psa 119:2, Eccles 3:6

After much searching, Geo arrived at the small opening in the great glass Dome Barrier to the Kingdom and was able to force the opening just wide enough to barely pass through with a mighty thrust!

Once making it down to the Kingdom floor, Geo did not recognize anything, for much time had passed. Times were good now, and after searching high and low for the king and queen, everyone now seemed to be like a king and queen, yet everyone seemed like a stranger.

Because of this, Geo put out an announcement throughout the Kingdom for anyone claiming to have lost a child during the Great Dome Barrier Quake of thirty years ago to come forward.

But unbeknownst to Geo, a lot of people had lost their children in the big Barrier Quake many years ago. Hundreds of people showed up to claim Geo.

"I have an idea," said Geo. "I remember my father's words. He said I would recognize him by his most valuable possessions. Surely, I will remember his fine clothing, or things from my childhood," Geo thought.

"All of you come back tomorrow and show me your most valuable possessions!" shouted Geo.

Psa 34:4, Psa 77:6

One by one, all of the Kingdom fathers returned with their most valuable possessions.

Since the king and queen were once great and powerful royalty in all of the land, only those having the greatest wealth and possessions would be allowed in to present their case. This would surely filter out and greatly narrow down the crowd to help find Geo's true father and mother.

As expected, there were tons of precious rubies, gold, diamonds, rings, watches, and clothes, along with deeds to mansions, cars, boats, condos and airplanes. Finally, after all of the fathers had presented their valuable possessions, Geo began to grow sad. Although some of the people were very kind, none of the fathers seemed to be recognizable. Geo began to weep.

"I'll never find my father and mother. I'll never see them again. I give up!" cried Geo.

Geo gratefully and politely sent out all the fathers from the room, then followed them outside, before sitting upon some steps, staring despondently at the ground.

From a distance, an older, bearded, common looking and modestly dressed man approached. The man asked for Geo's hand.

Geo looked up with confusion. "What is this, old friend? Do you need money? If you come back tomorrow, I will give you some. I will honor my word as my long-lost father had taught me. I don't want to be bothered right now. Please go away," pleaded Geo, as more tears began to flow.

Psa 55:2, Psa 69:29, John 16:20

Just then, the old gentleman reached out and placed a small pouch containing five stones in the palm of Geo's hand and then closed it.

Geo's eyes grew wide and a radiant smile followed. The stones looked very familiar.

"Father, it is you! Thank God!" shouted Geo. "These are the Father's Day stones I gave to you to keep for me…my precious stones from the Seas of Courage, Compassion, Confidence, Commitment, and Capability! I had to think about them often in order to make it through many a circumstance in my life."

"Weep no more," said the old man. We have alas found one another. I have found my Geo," rejoiced the old king.

"Why did you not come forward during the announcement?" asked Geo.

"I did, my child, but we had exhausted our wealth in search of you, and your rules would not allow me in, as I had only these stones in my pocket. Yet, they have always been my most valuable possessions. I tried to show them to you before you went up through the Dome Barrier that day, but it was too late. You had already gone," the king replied.

"How could I be so unwise, Father? I should have known what is most valuable to you has nothing to do with worldly possessions! Please forgive me, Father," begged Geo. "I am so sorry."

Luke 15:24

They happily embraced one another and started walking down toward the small cottage house together to greet mother, just like they had done so many years ago.

This time, it was the father who noticed a special looking stone on the ground, and bent down to pick it up.

"Don't be so hard on yourself, Geo. Open your hand," said the king, softly.

"What stone is this, Father?" asked Geo.

"This is a stone from the Sea of Wisdom…one you had not yet found…until today," said the old king.

Geo smiled, and looked humbly to the ground.

"Come, Geo. We have lots to catch up about," announced the king.

As they approached the cottage, Geo saw his mother standing outside, with joyful tears flowing and arms wide open, waiting to hug her child once again.

"This was a special day indeed," thought Geo.

…For it just so happened, coincidentally, Geo had returned on Father's Day.

THE END

Exo 31:3, Job 12:13, Luke 2:40, Col 2:3, 2 Tim 2:7

CPSIA information can be obtained
at www.ICGtesting.com
Printed in the USA
LVHW070204240521
688303LV00006B/76